Modern Soliloquy

Twig Tarver

BookLeaf Publishing

India | USA | UK

Presentation by *BookLeaf Publishing*

Web: www.bookleafpub.com

E-mail: info@bookleafpub.com

ISBN: 9789363309289

First edition 2024

To My Friends Cire, J.M., Evets, Asil, Ssej,

My Children Nhoj, Ttam, Ivaj, Derfla

And My Brothers Nad and Shoj

Panic

Racing thoughts,
Early morning.
Its getting hot,
An early warning.

Trying to stop spinning out
Without a doubt
I'm crashing now.

Life line,
Call me on this life line,
Save me from my own mind,
Give me a chance.
Give me a way out of this --

Panic
I'm feeling pretty manic
And the pressure's Messianic

Panic

Up a creek without a paddle
And the creek is oceanic

Panic

Not a boss,
So not vibing.
Way to close
To un-aliving.

You were in my dream last night
Thought you'd be a calming sight
But You fed me a poison lie
And that was when I choked and died --
And Panicked.

Greener Pastures

We used to be so tight.

Or so I thought,

We grew apart,

I broke your heart.

Back when it felt so right,

I tried so hard

To touch the stars

But fell so far.

And I hear you speak of me

Tenderly

In the streets

But when I call your phone

Nobody's there,

I only get a busy tone,

But I thought you should know;

I just want me and you and again.

Can we be me and you and again?

I just need me and you again.

Can we be two?

I know that's it my fault,

I know I walked away,

I know the grass is greener on the path to big
mistakes.

This time I'll walk my talk,

This time I'll make a way,

This time I'll find the words to say the things I wanna say.

I just want me and you and again.

Can we be me and you and agin?

I just need me and you again.

Can we be two?

Just Fine

I can still feel the gut punch

When I saw you with that long brown hair

Wearing those shorts you know I like

I swear you just come around to remind me of
what we'll never have

I still got it bad but I'm so done with that.

Usually I'd spiral, usually I'd unravel

Usually my night would end with me, a judge, a
gavel.

But I'm just gonna down my moscato

I know I'll feel in in the 'morrow

But tonight I'll be just fine.

I'm just gonna vibe to the ladies locking arms
and singing Landslide.

I'm gonna sing louder and dancer harder

And if they ask why

I'll say "because tonight I'm feeling just fine"

I'm gonna be just fine.

Should Be

I should be happy.

I should be vibing,

Living it up like I'm 20 from the beach.

It should be catchy,

This Laughing and wilding,

Posting them cuts so that everybody sees.

But when the suns out and there no sun shine,

When the LA vibes can't reach your mind --

It's gloomy in LA.

Past the glammed up smiles,

The Beach-y bods for miles,

Past the 15 secs of fame,

It's gloomy in LA.

When the rains inside

Where the pain can hide away,

It's gloomy in LA.

Flashes are snapping

And nobody's asking

How it must feel in the California heat,

Heat To be pretty

Iconically sexy

Hiding the cuts where nobody else can see

But...

Your Beauty

Your dagger
Heaves forth a wretched utterance
Suffocated with yearning,
Despair,
I am an ass forever chained
To your revolving mill.

A Special Kind of Yearning

I yearn to slumber in space
To awake in the Mariana Trench.
A universe anew,
A world apart from my own.

A Little Bit of Drowning

I drown in exceptions,
I suffocate in other's dreams.
Save me from these muted horizons,
Tether me to the ground.
Am I destined to this cycle?
Will expectations eternally thwart my wanting?
Oh, Dark Blue,
Thrash and throw me,
I welcome your brand upon my lungs.

A Tapestry of Souls

Flesh of my flesh,
Soul of my soul,
And yet --
You know not the knitting that wails deep within
The psyche of my mind.
I am in need,
Surpassing love into deep desire.
The waters of my deep
No longer whole without the essence of you.

A Memory

You face call to me.
A whisper from the pitch
I must not answer.
For the siren
Is bound to a dream.
You are gone.

Hail Mary

Read your hand into my depths
And pull me up to be with you.
Save me from myself.

A Thought

I may wake up to find
I have, indeed, made bed in Hades all this time.

A Mouse in His Trap

If Love escapes me
And Joy surrounds me
On the outskirts of this tower,
My hair an inch too short to touch the ground,
Have I truly been alive?

Swimming

Swimming
Swimming in a sea of -
Not quite despair
Not quite happiness
Not quite. And yet,
Swimming.
Eyes closed, unsure of up.
Legs kick, arms paddle.
If this is life, I am tired.
Not sad,
Not hopeful,
Simply tired.
And I swim.

To Feel or Not To Fell

Why is my feeling so deep?
Why cant I touch the bottom;
The waves of this Feeling, too high.
Why is the texture a rough tapestry scraping the
skin of my cheek?
To feel is to live.
To live is the jealousy of souls passed.
Then why is this feeling untouchable,
Murky,
Muddy,
Why does the spark of that coveted gift feel
cursed?

R.I.P.

My voice schemes.
The silent one
Confined to the four corners of my mind.
It invites Inspiration and splis it in half
Reveling as the pieces emit their final twitches,
Electric signals and pulses.
Nothing remains.
No bloom to fill the nose.
No color to court the eye.
Nothing but dark, cold, steel.
Steely eyes.
Steely blood that pools in vien
On it's way
To complete its task.
Life evades it's grasp.

Inspiration lies still.

Slipping Life Lines

I feel my grip slip on this life line
But Im holding on like I'll be just fine.
How do you make a statement true when
Everything is overwhelming you?
I try. I try.
What else can I do
When everybody's cruising
Everybody's taking
Everybody's choosing
Everybody's chasing
And I just wanna be fine
I just wanna be.

Took it all in and
Gave it all back
When your world is crashing
What can you ask if
I just wanna be fine
I just wanna be.

I feel my grip slip on my own mind
But I know that it will fix in no time.
How do you make a statement true when
Everything is terrorizing you?

Nothing is working
What else can I do—when—

Everybody's cruising
Everybody's taking
Everybody's choosing
Everybody's chasing
And I just wanna be fine
I just wanna be.

Took it all in and
Gave it all back.
When your world is crashing
What can you ask if
I just wanna be fine
I just wanna be.

Sippin'

Sipping on you
Feel likes bathing in the sunlight,
Dancing in the moonlight.
God, it set the mood right
Falling in them blue eyes.

Not a clue,
I didn't have it .
Wasn't prepared for
What was gonna happen.
When I met you
It was like that love from before wasn't love
anymore.

You want my heart
Its yours, you have it.
Getting prepared for
'Bout to start a habbit.
My favorite part --
It's the way you feel what I feel, and it sho'
feeling real.

Sipping on you
Feel like bathing in the sunlight,

Dancing in the moonlight.
God, it set the mood right
Falling in them blue eyes.

I don't even know why but
Tonight you looking so nice
And baby right on cue I -
I'm falling in them blue eyes.

One Sided

Monday morning and I'm finally home.
What a crazy weekend working out on the road.
Couldn't help but steal a glance when you didn't
notice
And I know,

I'm not what you're looking for.
And the truth is I'm feeling foolish.
Yeah the truth is I'm wanting more
And I'm starting to think you knew this.

It sucks to want you.
It suck to want to,
To want to love you
In a way I know I'll never get to.

It sucks to love you
When you don't love too.